The Ultimate Estate Planning Guide For Successful Business Owners

YOUR BUSINESS YOUR MONEY

Learn the Secrets That Will Make Your Business Last for Generations

MICHAEL MONTEFORTE JR., ESQ.

MONTEFORTE LAW, P.C.
FAMILY • LEGACY • SECURITY

400 Tradecenter, Suite 6890
Woburn, MA 01801

Phone: **978-657-7437**

WWW.MONTEFORTELAW.COM

Printed in the United States of America.

ISBN: 978-1-63385-419-2

Designed and published by
Word Association Publishers

205 Fifth Avenue
Tarentum, Pennsylvania 15084
www.wordassociation.com
1.800.827.7903

Dedication

This Book is dedicated to the hardworking staff at Monteforte Law, P.C. Thank you, Nicole and Ashley. Without your hard work and dedication, we never would have made it this far. I love you all.

Also by
Michael Monteforte Jr:

Planning Ahead:
Everything You Need to Know About
Estate Planning and Elder Law

The Long Game:
The Top Ten Reasons Why Your Massachusetts
Long-Term Care Application Will be Rejected

Contents

Learn About Mike 1

1. Introduction 7
2. Traits that Business Owners Have in Common 11
3. Estate Planning Solutions for Business Owners 23
4. Life Insurance 35
5. Business Succession Planning 45
6. More Complicated Family Situations 57
7. Long-term Care 65
8. Marketing for Business Owners 77
9. Final Thoughts 79

Learn About Mike

About Me...

For people that know me, they know I hate talking about myself. But I always get asked about myself and how I got into this field of work. With all of the specialized areas in the law, there are so many other fields I could have chosen, but for me, the real value was in estate planning and elder law. So, if you want to know why I chose these fields for my life's work, and what they mean to me, feel free to keep reading. If you want to just skip ahead to the real stuff, feel free to do that too! The first question I always get is:

Why do you do this work?

The answer is actually really simple, I do it for my family. More specifically, I do this work in honor of my grandparents. Although they have passed, their memory is a constant reminder to me about why I chose this work and how I got to where I am today.

When I first started my own firm, I was taking whatever cases came in the door. I did divorce, custody, real estate, probate, and so much more. Name it, and I've probably done it. During this time, my grandparents were getting older and it was best for them to move into an assisted living facility. My grandfather began to suffer from dementia and his symptoms were getting worse by the day. As we all know, the costs of long-term care are astronomical. My family and I had no choice but to sit and watch my grandparents' savings drain day by day just so they could afford to live comfortably.

I am the only lawyer in my family (although my daughter Gabby might join me someday), so naturally everyone was looking at me to see what I could do to help. I was being asked about my grandparents' legal rights and they hoped I would have all the answers. If I am being honest, *I didn't know the answers.*

It was at that moment when I realized I needed to get educated on elder law and estate planning. Estate planning always interested me in law school, but at the time I wasn't sure if it was a field I could make a living off of. With my grandparents financially suffering, I realized it was time to find out. I took this opportunity to educate myself and learn as much as I possibly could. I needed to find some way — any way — to help my family. So, I studied and attended continuing legal education. I sought out every resource and read every book. I kept doing this until I reached a point where I finally felt like I knew what I was talking about. In the process, I learned that estate planning is something I enjoyed learning about, and I began to love it.

I was able to help my grandparents some, but we were late to the game. There was only so much I could do at that point because they failed to pre-plan. I did what I could, as best as I could. My grandparents got to live their final days safely and comfortably and I am glad I had a small part in that. In return, I found my real passion. Estate planning is a challenging field and is always in a constant state of flux. The only way to be good at it is to constantly learn and seek education. Good thing I love a challenge, and a good book.

I also realized there is a serious need for elder law attorneys. People trying to navigate it on their own get lost very easily and find themselves down a deep, dark hole of no return. They simply just don't know where they went wrong and where to turn next. I like being the guy that can reach out and yell "I can help!"

That's why I do what I do and why I am so passionate about it. By helping others, in some small way, it's like I am helping my grandparents too and hopefully making them proud. I lost my grandfather in 2017 and my grandmother in 2019. As a token of his memory, my grandfather left me his gold ring. He received it as an award for his years as a baseball umpire for New England high school sports. I keep this ring in a display case in my office, where I can see it every day. In 2020, I started a scholarship in his name, Albert Iamelli, as a way to further honor his legacy.

It is not just the ring; my office is filled with little trinkets and gifts my grandparents gave me. When I was first starting out, I could barely afford the rent. Nanny and Papa would give me everything from chairs to a microwave oven just to help me out in any way they could. A long time has passed since then, but I can look at these items – the ring, the name-plate on my desk, the microware and more – and I feel the joy of when they were still here. They are at the forefront of my mind all the time, and I tailored our firm's Core Values around them as well.

I currently only accept cases in elder law and estate planning now. While I have resources and a vast referral network available for clients needing other forms of legal help, my focus gives me the greatest opportunity to provide extensive help to the clients that I believe need it the most. I have several books and written reports that I provide my clients, free of charge, to help educate them about estate planning and elder law in plain English. I also do several speaking engagements each year where I explain the subject in easy-to-understand language.

People come to me in hard, confusing times. They, or their parents, have worked all their lives to save money to be able to live on. These people want to be sure that they are able to leave behind a legacy for their families and not lose everything they have worked for to the tax man and to long-term care facilities. When I tell them I can help, the weight falls off their shoulders and they can breathe again. I get to watch their relief every time I say I can help, and that is the best part of my day.

My Family

I live in Wilmington, Massachusetts with my wife Jill, and in 2021 we will have been married for twenty years. We have two children, Gabriella and Michael, who are both in high school. Gabby dances competitively in many different forms of dance, and Michael plays high-level baseball as a catcher. In my spare time I love to travel with my family and show my children all the different parts of the world. I'm also a rabid fan of Boston sports. When I'm not travelling, watching sports with my family, or out to dinner with Jill, I'm reading books (I read about 50 books per year) and watching my kids. When I'm not travelling or watching sports with my family, I'm reading books (I read about 50 books per year). The rest of the time, you can find me watching Gabby at dance competitions and watching Mikey play baseball, which takes us all over the country.

Introduction

Who should read this book?

The answer is any business owner that wants to protect their assets, protect their family, and minimize taxes. Are you making over $100,000 per year and paying heavy taxes? Do you want to pass your business on to the next generation? Do you have a business succession plan in place? Regardless of whether you've done no estate planning, some estate planning, or lots of estate planning, this book will have something of value for you.

Let's be honest, there's nothing quite like owning your own business.

You make your own hours, you get to be the boss, and no one can tell you what to do (well, my wife might disagree, but no one at work can tell you what to do). You get to build something from the ground up, and if it succeeds, you feel the pride that comes with a dream that has been realized. It takes guts, determination and perseverance, and is therefore something that very few people ever try. If you've done it, then kudos to you! You are part of the small percentage of people that walked the tightrope without a net and made it to the other side. That's no small feat.

But it's not all rainbows and sunshine, is it? As a business owner, especially when you start out, you often have to wear many hats. You might be the boss, but you're also emptying the trash and licking stamps. You are responsible for rent, insurance, and equipment. If you have employees you have to hire, fire, and make payroll. You have to deal with vacation days, benefits, health insurance, conflicting personalities, and workplace drama.

When I first started out, I worked for a small firm in Lynn, Massachusetts, until I learned enough that I was ready to strike out on my own. I found a tiny office space near my house, rented it, and set out to buy computers and furniture. That was 2006, and I had a two-year-old daughter and a one-year-old son (today, Gabby is 16 and is getting her driver's license, and Michael is 15 and looking for colleges where he can play baseball). At the same time, I had my wife's never-ending belief in me, and her absolute certainty that I could do it and be a success. In all honesty, without her support, I'm not sure I would have the fortitude to try.

I operated on a shoestring. I bought my desk and chairs with my credit cards and prayed that I would have enough clients to be able to pay my rent. I would stare at the phone and literally beg, out loud, for it to ring. It was not an easy road, and although I'm in a much different position now than I was then, it's a road I'm still on. My business is successful, I have a nice office, a great staff, and most of the time more calls than I can handle. But I'm not done, and I still have a long way to go, and a long way to grow.

I've learned a lot along the way. First, business owners are a different breed. Most of the time, even if we work in different fields, we have more similarities than we have differences. We face unique challenges.

As an estate planner for many years, I've done planning for all types of people. Rich, not so rich, big families, singles, the Greatest Generation, millennials, and everything in between. I've found that estate planning for business owners is among the most important, and most misunderstood, planning there is. It's easy to screw up, if you don't know what you're doing. But if you do it right, it's among the most rewarding work that I do, and it often has the biggest impact on the client and their families – the potential to help my business-owner clients and their families in a huge way.

I've also found that business owners are often so busy that they can neglect their own planning. They spend so much time worrying about others and the day to day of running the business that they put their own personal needs, and sometimes their family's needs as well, on the backburner. I have to remind my business owner clients that their own planning is *as important as running the business, because it's done to protect their families.*

IT'S DONE TO PROTECT THEIR FAMILIES.

Business owners have to use special care to do their planning and do it right. Take it from a business owner, you don't want to mess this up!

1 Traits that Business Owners Have in Common

Business owners have a lot of specific estate planning challenges that are unique to someone that runs their own company. The estate plan for a business owner needs to reflect that fact, and it needs to take special consideration for the business owner's family, as well as the business itself.

While we know that no two business owners and no two businesses are the same, there are a lot of common traits that business owners have, and we can use those common traits to help design a general plan and format that will work for most business owners. We then go back and adjust that general plan and turn it into the specific plan solely for that particular client.

In my years of practice, I have noticed certain characteristics that successful business owners share. Let's start by taking a look at some of them. First, most successful business owners are smart. It's almost impossible to be a successful business owner without some sense of intelligence. Now, intelligence doesn't always mean the same as being educated. There are plenty of smart business owners that don't have a fancy education or any secondary education at all. But what they do know is that they need to hire the people who will make up for any shortcomings in their own education.

Another common trait is that most business owners are confident. Running a successful business is a risk, and as a general rule, confident people take risks. Business owners tend to be risk takers. Even though there is always a risk of failure, there has to be an inherent confidence that the business will succeed, or else the business owner would never embark on that road in the first place. But being confident doesn't mean that the business owner knows everything. Instead, they recognize what they know and *what they don't know*. Then, they hire or contract for people that fill in those blanks. This is something I've done personally as well – I know what I'm good at, and that's what I stick to, but then I hire people to do (1) the things I'm not good at, or (2) that I just don't want to do.

There is always a risk of failure when running a business. I've been running my business for going on 15 years now, and still there are the occasional months when I have my doubts about making our numbers. No matter how long you've been at it, there is always some risk involved, and successful business owners are the ones that are willing to take those risks. Most business owners are ambitious and goal oriented. The only real way to know if your business is succeeding is to set goals and try to achieve them. Being goal-oriented is what helps us to determine what "winning" looks like, and how to measure whether or not we get there. If we don't meet a goal that we have set, we have to examine the reasoning behind why we did not reach that goal.

Being ambitious about your goals, setting high standards, is another common trait among successful business owners. Anyone can set simple goals, but most successful business owners also set complex goals, both short-term and long-term goals. The long-term goals, by definition, take much more time and effort to achieve and they are the measures by which we determine whether or not our business is successful.

Most successful business owners are okay taking responsibility not just for themselves, but for others too. When we have employees, we realize that it's not just our own families whose necks are on the line, but also the livelihoods of our employees as well. I run a small business with four employees (as of November 2020, that is). Not only does our profitability affect my wife and my children, but it also provides the livelihood for my employees and their families. That is a lot of responsibility, and that is something that successful business owners will put onto their shoulders willingly and use it as motivation for success.

Most business owners are researchers – they never stop learning. That doesn't mean that they spend hours at the library. However, most successful business owners will at least do some research before making a decision. Whether it's a decision to hire a particular contractor, or to hire an employee, or what insurance company to use. Most successful business owners don't go blindly into making decisions and they take the time to learn a little bit about the subject of their decision, whether it's researching in the field of the business itself or investigating a vendor that might be hired to do work such as creating a website or handling marketing.

The last trait on our list of common factors amongst successful business owners is that most successful business owners are proactive. Proactive means they seek to take some action, as opposed to being acted upon. The successful business owner looks for opportunities and makes decisions to take advantage of those opportunities. They don't let things like the economy, or coronavirus, or economic downturns keep them from reaching their goals. Instead, they look for ways to leverage their environment into success.

THE MOST SUCCESSFUL BUSINESS OWNERS ARE PROACTIVE

While being a business owner can be stressful and may not be for everybody, running a successful business is a great source of pride and a great way to provide for your family. A profitable business can also help you give back to your community.

Those are some common *positive* traits shared by most successful business owners. That's the good stuff. But successful business owners share other things in common as well, and they aren't so positive.

2 The Unique Challenges that Business Owners Face

Business owners have unique problems, and those problems tend to be shared by most successful business owners. Yes, we share many of the same positive traits, but we also share the variety of problems and challenges that come with owning a business. These problems range from employee issues and insurance, to hiring and firing. The business owner is in a unique position, and their problems require specialized solutions. These unique problems, especially when it comes to estate planning, need to be addressed by a specialist who knows exactly how to tackle the various problems that business owners share.

Let's talk about what some of those shared problems are. And then we will get into some of the solutions.

One of the prevalent and most important shared problems among business owners is saving for retirement. Many of us, me included, have conjured up the image of ourselves doing the same job, at age 100, because we either don't know how to stop, or fear we won't ever have enough money to stop. There's no pension or company match for us.

When you work for yourself, you don't work for a big company that will set up a retirement plan for you, and you don't have a company that will match your contributions. Therefore, most business owners have to find their own way to save for retirement. They have to set up their own plans, they have to set up savings vehicles, and the funding of those plans rests solely on their own shoulders. No one is giving them a 401k match or a pension. Business owners have to solve the retirement problem themselves. Sadly, rather than solve the problem, many business owners neglect their own retirement, because it's easier to pretend the problem doesn't exist. Taking action is *hard*. And if you're working every day and aren't familiar with retirement savings and the logistics of it, and you don't have anyone to do it for you, then taking action is *really hard*.

Similar to retirement challenges, successful business owners also share in the challenge of paying for their children's college education. Most of the business owners that I know aren't rich. Most are upper middle class and earn a comfortable living, but they make too much money to qualify for financial aid for college. At the same time, they don't make enough money to write gigantic checks every semester for their children's tuition. It is therefore up to the business owner to figure out a way to save for their children's college and not do so in a way that it hurts their family's standard of living. You can't go broke trying to help your kids pay for school – that's just going to guarantee you'll be working until you're 100.

Another unique problem shared by successful business owners is planning for the succession of your business. If you were to pass away, what happens to your business? A successful business owner needs to have a plan in place that explicitly states exactly what will happen – with no gray area and no room for questions. Is your family going to take over? Could they take over even if they wanted to? Many service-related businesses such as plumbers, electricians, and even financial advisors and lawyers, require special licensing just to be able to operate. So, if something happens to the business owner and he or she doesn't have a licensed partner or a family member or adult-child to take over, then the business either needs to be sold or even closed down. It is paramount that a business owner's estate plan covers the succession of their business in circumstances ranging from retirement to an untimely death of the business owner.

Along with succession of the business to one's family or beneficiaries comes the complicated issue of employees. A business owner is responsible for the lives and families of his or her employees, and having some sort of succession plan in place would keep the employees either working or otherwise compensated if something were to happen to the business owner. The business owner also has to consider what type of employee benefits to offer, such as health insurance and retirement plans, so that the employees have a way to save for their futures as well.

Successful business owners not only have to be experts at their own disciplines such as law, or building homes, or electrical contracting, but they also have to know how to run a business. Everything from choosing a business entity type, to insurance, to taxes. They need to know how to handle marketing as well as be knowledgeable about things like payroll and wage laws. While employees have to learn their job and go to work every day and do that job, a successful business owner has to know how to provide the product or service that the business is known for, and at the same time know how to drum up business, market to customers or clients, and know how to handle the day to day problems and the payment of bills.

During my years of practice, I've met many business owners who were very skilled at their trade or profession, but they did not know how to run a business. The owners that succeeded were the ones that recognized this and either (1) made a steadfast effort to learn about business or (2) hired other employees or managers to help them run the business. At the same time, I saw skilled craftsmen whose businesses failed because even though they were great at their job, they didn't know how to handle running the business every day. Or how to market. You could be the greatest homebuilder in the world, but if no one knows you exist, you won't be building for anyone.

Among the biggest problems that are shared between successful business owners is taxes. Now there's a word that no one likes to hear. And yes, everyone has to deal with taxes, but business owners have to deal with taxes on several levels.

First, they have to look at the tax on their businesses (income, excise, real estate). Then they have to look at the taxes on their own income and whether or not they are subject to things like self-employment tax. At the same time, successful business owners have to also consider things like estate taxes, which are among the most misunderstood taxes out there. You don't want to mess this one up!

Here in Massachusetts, we have a fairly low threshold for estate taxes, and most business owners don't even realize that their estates would be subject to estate taxes in the tens of thousands of dollars, and in many cases, even hundreds of thousands of dollars. That's why when I advise business owners and put together estate plans for those business owners, I make sure that we address these tax issues. Otherwise, if something happened to the business owner, his or her family is the one left holding the bag and their assets or inheritance left behind is chewed up by these estate taxes. Put it this way, if your estate plan doesn't consider estate taxes, then get yourself a new plan, AND a new estate planning lawyer!

Business owners have very specific insurance needs. Like most people, they need life insurance to compensate their family if something were to happen to them. At the same time, there are numerous other types of insurance, such as workers' compensation insurance, and health insurance that the business needs as well.

If the business is a partnership or has more than one owner or manager, oftentimes the partners have failed to consider what would happen if one of them were to pass away. It's a common problem that I see week in and week out. In those situations, the business needs to have a Buy/Sell Agreement that determines what happens to one business owner's share if the other were to pass away.

Sadly, many business owners, and many estate planners, miss this one. If one partner dies, is there compensation for the business owner's family? Does the surviving business owner now own the entire company? Insurance plays into this, because most of these Buy/Sell Agreements are funded through life insurance. The life insurance policy makes sure that there is compensation both (1) for partners, and (2) for the business owner's family, if something were to happen to him or her.

We'll talk more specifics on these Buy/Sell Agreements later.

Our last common issue to go over is marketing. You have a duty, to yourself, your company, your employees, and your family, to be profitable. To be profitable, you need customers or clients. The only way that your potential customers will know that you exist is through your marketing efforts. Whether it's through newspapers, radio, print ads or internet and social media marketing, you need to make your products and services available to your target market. Many business owners miss this step, and simply think that if they provide good services, business will come. This is a complete fallacy. Even if your business is mostly through referral, that's still marketing.

YOU HAVE A DUTY TO BE PROFITABLE

I would argue that second only to being great at what you do, your marketing is the most important ingredient of your business. And it's among the hardest to get right. Proper marketing can turn your business from a break-even to high profitability. Getting my marketing right has caused my firm to grow more in the last two years than in the previous ten years combined. We can help you with that.

3 Estate Planning Solutions for Business Owners

Like the shared problems discussed in chapter two, we have many shared solutions that business owners can use to rectify those problems. With a little bit of help from an estate planner, a business owner can protect his business and his family, while at the same time minimizing any conflict over the fate of the business if she passes away.

Part I - Starting with the Basics: The Business Owner's Big Three

With most of our clients, we start out with what we call Monteforte Law's "Big Three". Our big three of estate planning is the Last Will and Testament, the durable power of attorney and the healthcare proxy.

We are often asked if everyone needs a will. And the real answer is no, there are some situations where a person might not need a will at all. However, business owners are different. Even if they don't own any other assets or any real estate, they need to have a Last Will and Testament in place to determine what happens to their business assets if they were to pass away.

Most people are familiar with what a Last Will and Testament is. The long and short of it is that your will is a set of instructions where you indicate what you want to happen to your property if you pass away. Those instructions are left for someone of your choosing to follow. That person you choose, previously referred to as an executor, is now referred to as a personal representative in Massachusetts.

You leave your Last Will and Testament as instructions for your personal representative, telling him or her how to handle your business and how to handle your property if you pass away. In its simplest terms, that's all a Last Will is: a list of step-by-step instructions that your personal representative has to follow.

The second item in our big three is the durable power of attorney. The durable power of attorney allows you to designate someone to make financial decisions for you and sign your name in the event that you can't do so for yourself. The power of attorney is called "durable" because it is meant to last, even if you become incapacitated. A regular power of attorney ends if you were to become incapacitated, such as through a stroke, an accident or Alzheimer's and dementia. But when we add language to make the power of attorney "durable", we are saying that we want that document and the authority it provides in your chosen person, who is often called your agent or your attorney-in-fact, to withstand your incapacitation.

A DURABLE POWER OF ATTORNEY IS DESIGNATES SOMEONE TO ACT ON YOUR BEHALF, WHEN YOU CAN'T

In fact, a durable power of attorney is designed specifically to cover that type of incapacitation. This is especially important for business owners. For example, I had a client that was in a car accident, and she ended up in a coma. The story has a happy ending because after several weeks she completely recovered. But in the meantime, while she was in the coma, there were a lot of issues. First, she was a single mother, and all of her assets were held in her name alone. That means there was no one with access to pay her bills. She was also a business owner, and there was no one with access to the company's finances, checks or records.

On the personal side, we had the bank asking where the mortgage payments were, and we had the utility companies demanding payment. And this all happened in less than a 60-day period. She had plenty of money in the bank, but we had no way to access it. Her mother came to see me, and her mother had no way to access the personal funds or the business funds. So, her personal bills were not being paid, including her mortgage, credit card and utilities, and it was starting to affect her credit rating. At the same time, there were outstanding business bills, and she did not have a partner or anyone else with access to the business accounts. We were getting hit on both fronts. And those were just the bills we knew about. We were in a mad scramble trying to find records of what business bills were even in play. Because she did not have a durable power of attorney, we were making plans for her mother to file for a guardianship and conservatorship through the court, which is a lengthy and expensive process. Without a durable power of attorney, that's the only way to gain control over someone else's assets.

That process requires court hearings and testimony of medical experts. If she had a durable power of attorney in place, her mother could have taken that document to the bank and made sure that the personal bills got paid. She could have also accessed the business accounts and paid business bills as well. Instead of having to go through a court process that costs thousands of dollars and can take months, the whole problem could have been solved with a durable power of attorney, and it would have taken care of the whole mess.

With that one key document in hand, the person that you designate as your power of attorney can talk to banks, insurance companies, retirement companies, business contacts, and accountants. Therefore, it is, obviously, absolutely essential that the business owner have one. Without it, there's no company that will speak to anyone acting on your behalf.

The last document in our big three is the healthcare proxy. While this document is not necessarily specific to business owners, it is something that everyone should have regardless. The healthcare proxy allows you to designate someone to make healthcare decisions for you in the event that you can't do so for yourself. So, it's like a power of attorney for your healthcare. If you are incapacitated from an accident, or from dementia or Alzheimer's, the healthcare proxy allows you to name someone who can make decisions on your behalf. The idea is that while they would act in your best interest, they would also act in accordance with YOUR wishes (as opposed to their own, or those of another family member).

That way, there is no argument between family members regarding who should make these decisions. A good healthcare proxy document should include a number of ancillary documents that provide guidance to the healthcare agent that you designate. For example, the ancillary documents should state your wishes regarding being kept alive on respirators and feeding tubes in the event of an accident where you became brain dead or were going to be in a permanent vegetative state. While it's not a fun subject to talk about "pulling the plug" it's something that can lead to major strife within a family, if the person's wishes aren't clear. It's a lot easier for a health care proxy to enforce your decision, as opposed to having to actually make the decisions themselves.

The ancillary documents should also include preferences for your burial, cremation or services. They should include waivers to allow your doctors to speak to your healthcare agent without fearing any issues with patient privacy laws and HIPAA regulations. A good healthcare proxy document should include documentation about your preferences if you ever were to suffer from dementia, and what your wishes would be regarding your healthcare, feeding, personal hygiene and medications.

Those Big Three documents form the basis of almost any estate plan that we do. And they are essential for business owners, especially the durable power of attorney. Any additional planning builds off of those three documents, and the pieces have to work together like a jigsaw puzzle.

Part II
Let's Talk about Trusts Baby

There are hundreds of types of Trusts for hundreds of different purposes, but there are some Trusts that are especially effective and useful for business owners. Most of those Trusts have to do with protection from estate taxes. But before we get into estate tax protection Trusts, let's talk a little bit about family Trusts.

The Family Trust

A family Trust is where you leave your assets to chosen beneficiaries, but they are held in Trust pending the happening of certain events, for example, the beneficiary reaching a certain age, or completing his or her college education. In the case of a married couple with children under 18, typically the spouses named each other as beneficiaries of the Trust, and their children as the secondary beneficiaries. That means that one's assets would pass to their spouse. And if their spouse passes away or predeceased them, the children would be next in line to receive the assets. But the great thing about family Trusts is they allow us to leave assets over time instead of all at once.

If you pass away and leave everything to your children, and they are minors, their guardian has completed unfettered access to the funds with no oversight.

What is potentially even worse is that the day the child becomes 18, he or she will inherit the funds and have control over everything. As of right now in 2021, I have two young children. My daughter is 16 and my son is 15. I absolutely know 100% that I would not want my son to inherit the estate from my wife and me when he turns 18 because he would spend the money on fancy sports cars and have nothing left to put himself through college. If something ever happened to my wife and me and we didn't have a Trust in place, I can almost guarantee you'd see him tearing up the streets of Massachusetts in a Ferrari or something equally loud. That's the beauty of the family Trust. It allows you to name someone else to hold the purse strings, and that person is called the trustee.

The trustee uses the money for the children's benefit until they reach certain benchmark ages that you select. Then the money is disbursed to the children over time so that they can learn how to manage it. Typically, we divide the assets into three pieces, and we may give them one third at age 18 or 21, the second third at age 23, and the final third at age 25. But the ages can be anything that you choose. Sometimes I have clients that tell me their kids can't have control of the money until they are 50!

The family Trust can also help protect the money from liabilities. Likewise, if your children were to marry young and divorce young, undispersed Trust funds can be protected from becoming marital assets and therefore wouldn't be divided in a divorce. This Trust needn't be used solely for cash assets; assets of a business or even shares of the business owner's company stock can be left to the children this way as well. The family Trust solves a lot of problems when your children are minors, but we can modify the family Trust to also include estate tax savings provisions. When we add these estate tax provisions to a family Trust, we have changed the fundamental nature of the Trust, and it becomes what we call a <u>credit shelter Trust</u>.

The Credit Shelter Trust

Yes, it includes the same family Trust provisions, but it has additional language to help minimize estate taxes for a married couple. Right now in Massachusetts the estate tax threshold is $1 million. Most people think that is a big number because most of us are not millionaires. However, that number includes not just your assets, but your retirement and your life insurance payouts as well. For example, I have a $1 million life insurance policy so that if anything happens to me, my wife and children are taken care of. If I die, just by virtue of that policy alone, I am already over the Massachusetts estate tax threshold before we even look at any of my other assets. And what's even more fun is that, if you're over the $1 Million threshold, your estate taxes don't start taxing the overage, oh no, instead, you are taxed back from the first dollar!

In Massachusetts, if I die and leave everything to my spouse, my $1 million estate tax exemption that every person in Massachusetts is entitled to dies with me. However, if we insert the credit shelter Trust into play, that Trust preserves my $1 million tax exemption from estate taxes, while still allowing my spouse complete access to the money.

If done right, married couples should be able to have $2 million in assets and not owe any estate taxes, and even without proper planning, you can avoid the estate tax at the passing of the first spouse. But at the passing of the second spouse, a heavy estate tax can be incurred, and it leaves a huge bill for the children. The money to pay the tax is taken out of what should be their inheritance. The estate taxes can easily reach six figures!

The credit shelter Trust helps us prevent that by preserving each spouse's $1 million exemption. Remember that the gross taxable estate includes all of your assets such as bank accounts, retirement, and life insurance payouts, but it also includes business assets and the value of business stock. For business owners, they can very easily go over the Massachusetts threshold. If there is not sufficient money in the estate as far as liquid cash to pay the estate tax bill, the business might even need to be sold or have its assets sold just to pay the estate tax bill.

IF DONE RIGHT MARRIED COUPLES CAN HAVE $2 MIL. IN ASSETS AND NOT OWE ANY ESTATE TAXES

The credit shelter Trust helps knock down that estate tax number. And in many cases, it eliminates the estate tax altogether. As a business owner,

I know that I don't want to see my business assets sold off to pay taxes!

While we do recommend credit shelter Trusts for a lot of married couples, business owners are in the unique position where they can take huge benefit from it, and they can pay huge penalties without it. I mentioned my own personal life insurance policies, and that is a good segue into our next section that centers on life insurance as a way to deal with estate taxes and other special insurance considerations for business owners.

The Irrevocable Life Insurance Trust (ILIT)

As a licensed life insurance broker, I have been trained to evaluate a client's particular situation with regard to life insurance policies and how they may benefit the client. For business owners, life insurance has many functions, but first let's look at the effect of life insurance on estate taxes.

Before we get into different types of life insurance and their benefits to business owners, let's just talk about life insurance death benefits. When it comes to estate taxes, there's nothing that can put you over the limit faster than life insurance. Again, I use myself as an example. I have a house, some bank accounts, and some retirement, but I have a million dollar life insurance policy. It makes sense for me, as the primary earner in my family, and when I die, that million dollars goes to my wife and kids to make sure they are taken care of, but the government is going to look at that death benefit and include it in my taxable estate. It seems weird, because we don't actually realize that death benefit *until we die*, but the government doesn't care, and they count it in your gross taxable estate. So before I even get into calculating my other assets, the life insurance has me *over the Massachusetts limit* and estate taxes will be due.

In cases where life insurance death benefits are the primary cause for putting you over the top of the Massachusetts estate tax threshold, we can introduce the Life Insurance Trust; we called it an ILIT (Irrevocable Life Insurance Trust). When done correctly, this life insurance Trust can pull the value of your life insurance death benefit *out* of your taxable estate. It's an extremely useful tool, and it is especially important for business owners because most successful business owners have several different life insurance products. With the ILIT we can literally pull millions out of the taxable estate, and with it, tens and even hundreds of thousands of dollars in estate taxes!

There are rules of course. If you create a new policy and make the life insurance Trust the owner from the outset, then the value of the death benefit is immediately removed from the taxable estate. If instead, we are taking an existing life insurance policy and changing ownership over to the life insurance Trust, then it takes three years to be fully effective. Therefore, the best way to do it is at the inception when you take out the policy, but it can still be done afterwards as well, and is protected in three years. If we are able to successfully remove the amount of the death benefit from your taxable estate, then we can look at the rest of the assets, and using a combination of vehicles like the credit shelter Trust, we can oftentimes cut the estate tax down to zero. For example, we should be able to take a married couple with $2 Million in combined assets and $2 Million in life insurance and reduce the estate tax that would be over $280,000 all the way to zero!

4 Life Insurance
as a business owner, yes, you definitely need it, for more reasons than you think

Part I
Using (cheap) term life insurance to pay estate taxes

What about cases where we cannot cut the estate taxes all the way down to zero? What if the assets are too high, to the point where we know there's going to be at least *some* estate tax? In those cases, we can use inexpensive life insurance policies, such as term life insurance, and the death benefit for those policies can be used specifically to pay for estate taxes. A term life insurance for $50,000 or $100,000 can cost a few dollars a month. It's very cheap, and the death benefit can be earmarked specifically for payment of the estate taxes.

That's why when choosing an estate planning attorney, it is important that you choose someone who specializes in estate planning, but it's also important they know about life insurance as well. When a client comes to my firm, we look at their overall estate tax picture and figure out if we can completely cut out all estate taxes and reduce the number to zero. In the event that we cannot cut it to zero, then we determine the potential amount of estate taxes and look into cheap term life insurance policies to pay those taxes. With a term life insurance policy like that, you can obtain $100,000 in death benefit, for very low cost. Sure, over the entire term of the policy, the costs typically range in the few thousands of dollars, but the death benefit can pay a $100,000 estate tax bill. It's certainly a fair trade. That way we aren't taking away from your family's inheritance in order to pay those taxes.

Part II

Retirement through whole life insurance policies and traditional retirement savings (we don't get a match)

Let's change gears and talk about other types of life insurance. It's great being a business owner for so many reasons. It's great to be your own boss and use your time any way you like to. No one tells you what to do or sets your schedule, and you get to be in charge. But there are lots of pitfalls that business owners can slip into if they are not careful. Many of those pitfalls have to do with retirement savings. Unlike being an employee at a big company, business owners don't have anyone to offer them retirement benefits. There's no big corporation offering us a 401(k) with some type of dollar match.

And yes, we can set up our own retirement plans through our business and have the company match our personal contributions. But let's be real about it. The money from the company is still really money from us. We are using our own money to match ourselves. While there's nothing wrong with that, it's not the same as having a company pay to match your retirement benefits.

Likewise, there's nobody to give us a pension. There's no corporation or business entity that's going to continue paying a percentage of our salary for the rest of our lives. Retirement savings is 100% on us. As a business owner, it's very easy to get caught up in the day to day and then a month to month frame of thinking where we are concentrating on making that month's bills, paying that month's payroll, and taking home that month's profits. With that type of mentality, it's very easy to continually put off planning for the future. When there's no company 401(k) match and no company pension, most business owners don't even know where to start.

As a side note, many payroll companies offer retirement plan services, both for yourself and for employees. If your payroll company offers that type of benefit, it's an easy way to incorporate it into your business and to have an added benefit to help attract and retain great employees.

But still, where does that leave us? Maybe with a 401(k) or IRA that we have to fund ourselves, but then what? How else can we finance our retirement, when we don't have a pension that will pay us income during our retirement? Enter the whole life insurance policy – it provides more than just a death benefit. A whole life insurance policy can be used to design a pension for yourself.

Now, we are not talking about cheap term life insurance anymore. Here we are talking about whole life policies, and whole life policies are a lot more expensive because they never expire. It's different with a term policy. If you have a 20 year term life insurance policy and you pay into that policy for 20 years and you don't die, then the policy ends and the insurance company has collected 20 years' worth of payments from you and has not paid out a dime. There is no cash value and no death benefit if you survive past the term. Policies like that are great if you're talking about a death benefit for a loved one or a way to pay for estate taxes, but they do not make good retirement vehicles. However, because whole life policies never expire, there *has* to be a payout at some point, either after a number of years or at your death. And that means the life insurance company is going to charge a lot more for it.

A properly drafted whole life policy can be used to pay out monthly income upon your retirement. In fact, a policy like this can provide a completely accurate upfront illustration so that you know exactly what you need to pay in and exactly how much you will get out when it comes time to start collecting. I personally have one of these policies, and I've been paying into it for several years. If you pass away prior to retirement,

A WHOLE LIFE POLICY CAN BE USED TO PAY OUT MONTHLY INCOME UPON RETIREMENT.

your family gets the death benefit, but if you survive into retirement, you can start drawing off the cash value every month and you can even take loans against the policy. It's a more expensive product, sure. But when used properly, it can satisfy a huge need that most business owners have.

My biggest regret is not starting it sooner when my business was newer. It's expensive, but I should have found a way to do it because the payouts in my retirement would have been that much higher. Regardless, I am contributing to one of these policies now, and when I retire, it will provide me monthly income that should last me the rest of my life.

The other important thing is that these policies have a guaranteed rate of return. Sure, you can invest your money in the stock market and you should do so, but there are not any mutual funds or stocks out there that guarantee anything. They don't guarantee a particular rate of return at all and are subject, of course, to losses as the market goes up and down. These whole life policies can be designed so that you never lose the money that you put in and with illustrations to clearly tell you the minimum that you will get out of the policy when you start drawing from it. It is a huge mistake for business owners to overlook these policies.

Oftentimes people are scared by the term "whole life policy" because they know that it costs more than a term policy, but in this case, you do get what you pay for. They don't come cheap, but what good thing ever does? Not enough business owners know about this tactic, so they don't take advantage of it. It's a must-do.

Part III
College savings through whole life

We've already talked about using life insurance as a way to pay estate taxes and as a way to create retirement savings and pensions. But another use for whole life policies, especially for business owners, is to create and grow college savings for our kids. Here is yet another solution that I learned too late in life and wish I had started earlier.

You can set up whole life policies under your children's names and contribute to those policies over time. The cash value and the guaranteed growth of the policy can be used as college savings. Just as with whole life savings for retirement, you can receive clear illustrations of exactly what the policy will be worth and when, and you will know exactly how much money will be in there for your kid's college when they turn 18 and graduate from high school. You will also know exactly how much you need to contribute if you want to have a certain amount of savings. Obviously the earlier you start contributing to these policies, the more money that's in the accounts when they turn 18, so that the funds can then be applied for tuition, fees, room and board, and other college expenses.

For business owners, again, we get focused on a monthly or even quarterly mentality. We need to pay that month's bills, make payroll and take home our profits. But there isn't always a lot of focus on savings for retirement and other things like our children's educations. These whole life policies for kids are relatively cheap – even more so than a whole life used as a "pension". You can set the amount that you want to contribute to them and grow college savings that way. You can change the amount of contributions over time, if you wish, but your insurance broker should be able to show you, based on your child's age, exactly how much you would need to contribute each year if you want them to have a certain amount saved by the time they are graduating. The growth is guaranteed, and not as tied to the market as something like college saving through a government 529 Plan. Those government plans aren't a bad thing, but they fluctuate with the market, and don't have guaranteed growth. There's nothing wrong with having both the insurance and a 529 Plan account, but the 529 Plan by itself is definitely not the answer. The whole life is predictable, while 529 savings are not – more on this below.

If you are not looking to have a pre-set dollar amount by the time they turn 18, and you would just want to have *some* college savings for them, you can set a monthly contribution of your choosing and it will grow until it's time for the child to cash it out and use the money for school. Even if you can only afford a small contribution, the guaranteed growth will make the most out of what you can afford to contribute.

You can contribute a little, or you can contribute a lot, or you can contribute based on a certain target amount of dollars. Again, you can change the amount of your contributions over time. And if you start this plan when your child is young enough, you can make for huge savings that can be put toward your kid's tuition. I have policies like this for both of my children, who right now (in 2021) are aged 16 and 15. My daughter is a junior in high school, and my son is a sophomore in high school. My only regret with regard to these policies is that I did not find a way to start them sooner. I subscribed to the conventional wisdom that I just couldn't afford it.

What I didn't realize was that I could contribute any amount I wanted to these policies and at least get them started when my kids were very young. Instead, I started it much later and if I want to pay for my kid's college, it means that there will be much more money that I'm going to have to pay out of pocket when the time comes - in another two years, for me.

People often ask if 529 plans offer a better savings vehicle than the whole life, but I don't think so. Right now, I do have both, but the life insurance option is superior in many ways. I have 529s for my kids, and I have these policies for my kids, but I contribute more to the policies. A 529 plan is based on the market, and the value in those plans will increase or decrease with the market. This year, 2021, coming off the year of the pandemic, my 529 plans haven't gained a dime, and are at a net loss for the year. The 529 plans give me no investment choices, because they are state-run, so I have no control over the investments and no way to change them. Therefore, if the market is tanking, all I can do is watch the value plummet. You can lose huge amounts of money that you put in there, and your investment isn't safe, with no guaranteed minimum and no protection for the contributions you make. While I do have these 529 plans for both of my kids, I contribute a small amount there. The whole life policy option is much different in that they have minimum guarantees. In other words, you can't lose what you put in. They are not market-based, and they have a set rate of return that is easily trackable.

If you put $1,000 into a 529 plan, then in a year, you might have $1,200, or you might have $800. If you put $1,000 in one of these whole life policies, then in a year, you will, at the very least, have that $1,000 that you put in, plus the guaranteed gains that the policy promises.

The reason why these policies can be especially useful for business owners is because business owners are not likely to get much financial aid. Yes, there is financial aid that is based on grades and athletics, but the primary financial aid available, especially through federal programs, is need-based. And let's face it, most business owners are not going to qualify for need-based financial aid.

The government looks at the income from the business and quickly determines that you make too much money and disqualify you right off the bat from need-based financial aid. That means you've got to pick up the tab yourself to whatever degree you're planning on helping your kids with college. And these whole life policies are a great way to do it at relatively low cost. There is a policy to fit every budget.

There is another major upside for these whole life policies versus a 529 plan, and that is the limitations on what can be done with the money from 529 plans. What if your child decides not to go to college? Or decides to go to a trade high school instead? Because the 529 plan is a creation of federal statute, it has very specific uses that can be made of the funds in those accounts. Yes, they can be used to pay for post-secondary education, but if your child is not going to college, they're limited in what they can do with this money.

That is not so with the savings in these whole life policies. The cash value in the whole life policies can be used to pay for college. But if your child doesn't go to college, then those funds are not limited in any way as far as their use. When the child turns 18, you can give the policy to the child and let them cash it out and take the money to for some other purpose. They can continue to pay into the policy themselves and have cash value continue to grow for additional years and use that money down the road for something like a wedding or buying their first home. There's no question that the whole life policy is more versatile than the 529.

There are no limitations on what can be done with the whole life policy cash value, which is why it can be particularly useful to business owners. Sometimes it makes sense for our children to follow in our footsteps and either join in, or take over, our business. In those cases, it's possible that a college degree is required, but in other cases, it's not. The child could use that money for getting started in the business and pay for things like licensing and equipment.

THERE ARE NO LIMITATIONS ON WHAT CAN BE DONE WITH THE WHOLE LIFE POLICY CASH VALUE

Regardless of their ultimate use, these policies create a nice nest egg that can help the child get off to a great start in life, as opposed to the 529 cash, which carries with it specific use and numerous limitations. Again, I think it's wise to do both, but if I were choosing one or the other, there's no question that the 529 would take a back seat to the whole life.

5 Business Succession Planning

Business owners have to take special care with their estate planning because they have to deal with business succession. In other words, what happens to the business if you pass away? Many business owners neglect to put succession planning in place, and then if they pass away, it leaves a complete mess for their families. There's no indication about what's to be done with the business, how ownership and management is supposed to change, or whether the business is to continue or be sold after the business owner's death.

Succession planning depends on whether the business is owned and run by one person versus a business owned and run by several partners. The other difference-maker is what type of entity the business is organized as, whether it's a sole proprietorship, a corporation or a limited liability company, (LLC).

There are other considerations, all related to the business owner's specific circumstances: Are there children? Are they minors? If so, is there a family Trust to disburse the business interests to the children? What about the conclusion for the shares of the company? Are the kids going to sell? What about when they are older - will they take over? In the service industry, the customer is buying "you". Is there still a value if you're not there? If the kids are older and take over, a client might not mind buying from your kids. But if the kids are young, can the business be sold? Or kept? Who runs it?

All of these questions should be answered by your succession plan. Whether your succession plan is part of your Will and a Trust, or part of a Buy/Sell Agreement, it has to be part of your overall estate plan. Many estate planners neglect this, even supposed "specialists", and it's quite possibly the most crucial part to your plan.

The plan for an individual business owner has to be very different from a plan for if you have partners. If you pass away, then what? Is there a Buy/Sell Agreement in place? If so, what kind: one type of Buy/Sell pays your family cash compensation while the surviving partner keeps the business, and the other kind of Buy/Sell pays your partner a cash-out benefit so that the loss is covered, and your family gets your shares. There's even a third kind of Buy/Sell that is a hybrid combination of the two. How do you know the right kind? Well, that's what your estate planning lawyer should tell you.

Don't forget that your plan needs to change with time, especially if you have young children; it may need to be modified when the kids grow up. When they are minors, it might be better to have them get the money instead of the shares. But when they are older, the shares might make sense.

Part I
Succession Planning for Different Types of Business Entities

Businesses come in all different shapes and sizes. From a one-person show to corporations with multiple employees, they all need a succession plan. But the plan can differ, depending on the size of the company.

Single Owner Entities

First let's look at a sole proprietorship. Under a sole proprietorship model of business, we've got one owner, and no legal business entity. Instead, the individual owner is doing business in his/her own name. There are no corporate shares. There is no LLC percentage of ownership interest. Instead, the business owner owns 100% of the company and files taxes and accounts under his or her own social security number. In the case of a sole proprietorship, unless the business deals with the company in his Last Will, then the ownership of the company could pass to his state-determined beneficiaries, which could include a spouse or children or a combination of the two.

First, we have to look at what type of business the sole proprietorship is. If the sole proprietor passes away, then what happens to the company? Part of that answer depends on licensing. For example, if the sole proprietor is a licensed electrician, but his spouse and children are not licensed electricians, then what happens to the company when he passes away? In those cases, the business most likely has to be sold because there are no family members to take over. This can be specified in a business owner's Will so that there is a clear indication of what is to be done. If the sole proprietor has family members that are also electricians, then one of those electricians might want to take over the business. But in that case, what then happens to the non-electrician family members?

A failure to designate the specific succession plan in the Will can lead to many problems. Take our electrician business owner example, but say we now have another electrician who is the son of the electrician sole proprietor that passed away, and he may think that he will step in and the business will belong to him. This is especially likely if he worked with his father for a long time, and if there are no other electricians in the family. But what about the spouse and other children who are not electricians? They would receive no share of the business if the sole proprietor's electrician son took over 100% ownership. That may or may not be what the sole proprietor was planning. And that's why he has to state as such in his Will.

Perhaps the intention was to have the electrician son *buy out* the other family members so that they receive an inheritance, and the electrician son takes over the business. Or what if the electrician son was vital in growing the business and has been working there for several years? In that case, the sole-proprietor may not want other children to receive a share of the business. Without a Last Will and Testament to indicate what's to happen, the family members are left guessing, and very often they are left fighting. It is therefore imperative that the sole proprietor have a Last Will and Testament in place.

Now let's look at corporations. Corporations come in two forms: S corporations and C corporations. S-corps are small businesses, and c-corps tend to be larger companies. For succession planning purposes, both of those types of corporations rely on shares of stock. The corporation has a certain number of stock shares that have been issued and if there is only one owner, that owner is the holder of all the stock. What happens if there's one owner of the shares, and that owner passes away? Where does the stock go? If it is designated in the owner's Last Will, then there are clear instructions about whether the stock shares are to pass to family members, whether or not the stock shares are to be sold, or whether someone else in the family might be inheriting the shares and taking over the business.

We have the same issues here as we do with sole proprietorships in that the business might be the type that anyone can take over without any licensing, such as ownership of a retail store or food store. But if the corporation hinges on licensing such as an electrician or a CPA or a lawyer, then it can only be taken over by an individual that holds the correct licensing. In those cases, what happens to the shares? Are family members supposed to buy each other out or are the shares to be sold by the stock owner's executor and the funds dispersed to the family? Again, it is imperative that a Last Will and Testament be put in place to answer these questions.

Lastly, looking at the limited liability company or LLC, the ownership is not held through shares. Instead, an LLC ownership is held through a percentage interest. If we've got one owner, then that owner holds 100% of the ownership interest in the LLC. Again, in that case, if the owner were to pass away, what happens to the ownership interest in that LLC? Is it split up amongst the beneficiaries or is the ownership interest to be sold to a third party? And again, the same issue arises as to whether licensing is required for running the business and whether or not there is a licensed individual in the family that would take over. If so, are the other family members to be compensated so that they are not shortchanged from a share of their family member's business? The estate plan should address this.

Part II
Multiple Owner Entities

If the business is organized with more than one owner, whether it's a partnership or a corporation with multiple stock owners or an LLC with multiple owners of the percentage interest, it is even more vital that a Last Will and Testament be put in place. Similarly, there should be a partnership agreement or an LLC operating agreement or corporate bylaws that can also state what will happen if one of the owners passes away.

If two owners each have a 50% interest in a company, regardless of what type of company it is, and one of the owners passes away, then what happens? Does the remaining owner take over and own 100% of the company now? Well then what about the deceased owner's family? Do they get nothing? Does the owner want his 50% share to go to his family so that they can take part in the business as 50% owners, or does the surviving owner have a right of first refusal to buy out the deceased owner's family and become the sole 100% owner? These issues have to be contemplated in both the owner's estate planning and in their business documents. Without it, the resulting chaos can bankrupt the business.

If there is no succession strategy named in the partnership agreement or other corporate or LLC agreements, it can lead to major problems if one of the owners passes away. Naturally the deceased owner's beneficiaries are expecting their share, but is it even a type of business that they could run if they wanted to? And even if it is the type of business they could be involved in if they wanted to, does the surviving owner want new partners?

It is vitally important that partners, regardless of whether it's two partners, three partners or more, in any of these business entities, discuss the succession plan and set out the instructions for if one of them were to pass away. It has to be in writing, and a proper legal format. A handshake agreement means nothing, and I've seen multi-million-dollar companies rely on them, only to have that agreement crumble.

NO SUCCESSION STRATEGY NAMED IN THE PARTNERSHIP AGREEMENT CAN RESULT IN CHAOS

It's possible that the surviving business owner has no desire to be in in a partnership with the deceased owner's family. She may insist on buying them out, but in that case, who sets the value? Is an appraisal done so that the deceased owner's family isn't short-changed? And in cases of many small businesses, if there were to be a buyout, can the surviving owner even afford to buy out the deceased donor's family?

These problems and questions can all be answered with complete and detailed business succession documents. While a Last Will and Testament plays a big part in this, as can be the case with a family Trust, a Buy/Sell Agreement is also essential.

Part III
Buy/Sell Agreements with Life Insurance

Unexpected deaths happen every day. We've all seen the havoc that covid-19 wreaked upon all of our lives this year. Still, most people think they have plenty of time. In my line of work, I see it every day, that no one is promised tomorrow. We therefore have to plan, with our families, and our business partners, for tragic events, instead of blindly believing "it won't happen to me". That mentality is an act of cowardice.

I've seen it many, many times when one partner passes away and it turns into a dispute and even litigation between the deceased owner's family and the surviving partner. That's because in these cases, the partners did not put their wishes in writing. They did not discuss, agree upon, and put a succession plan in writing, and they did not put together an estate plan that would deal with these issues. That leaves the deceased person's beneficiaries and the surviving partner left to argue about what is supposed to happen, what's fair and what represents adequate compensation.

On top of the big three that we recommend for business owners and for most people in general, we have to include number one, succession planning, which is made part of that big three through the Last Will and Testament, and number two, a Buy/Sell Agreement that clearly designates the terms between the partners so that everyone has clear notice of what has been agreed upon and what is to happen if one owner passes away. That includes how the shares would be treated, how they would be valued and whether or not there are any rights of first refusal to surviving partners.

Even if the partners had made an agreement about a buyout, where does the money for the buyout come from? That's where we get into what are called Buy/Sell Agreements between the partners.

A Buy/Sell Agreement is a written contract between owners of a company where it is explicitly stated as to what happens when one of the partners passes away. It can state that the deceased owner's share goes to his family via stock or ownership interests, and/or that his family has the right to step into his shoes and be a partner in the business. Or it may specify that the percentage ownership of the deceased person passes to the surviving partner, but that the surviving partner is then to monetarily compensate the deceased owner's family. But how is that to be decided? Well, the terms are set forth in the Buy/Sell Agreement, including methods for appraisal if there is dispute about the company's value.

Very often these Buy/Sell Agreements are funded with life insurance.

In the case of an owner passing away, and the surviving owner or owners are taking over the business, with a payout to the deceased's family, where does the money come from? If the company does not have the cash to pay for a buyout, which most do not, then life insurance can be used to fund the buyout.

These Buy/Sell Agreements can be funded through relatively inexpensive life insurance policies. Then after the passing of the partner, the life insurance death benefit can compensate either the remaining partners or the deceased partner's family so that the business can continue, and no one is short-changed.

The partners can take individual policies or joint policies that can be paid for by the company, making it a business expense, and in some cases tax-deductible. If one of the owners passes away, the Buy/Sell Agreement could specify that the death benefit from the life insurance passes to the deceased owner's family as compensation, and that the surviving owner takes over as 100% owner of the business. This can work with any entity type, regardless of whether we are talking about corporate stock shares, or LLC ownership interest. In the alternative, the Agreement could also specify that the shares go to the deceased owner's family and that the life insurance death benefit is paid to the surviving owner as compensation for the loss to the company, to either hire new personnel or otherwise compensate for the loss of the first partner that has passed away.

As is the case with many small businesses, especially businesses with only two or three owners, each owner takes an equal share in the daily work and in the goods or services provided. So, if one passes away, it can literally cripple the business. Having a life insurance policy in place to either compensate the remaining owners or compensate the deceased owner's family so that the remaining owners take over the deceased person's share of ownership, is critical to proper succession planning for the business.

Succession planning can change over time, and be modified as the partners age, or as their beneficiary's age. For example, planning for owners with children who are under 18 should be vastly different from planning for owners who have adult children. Adult children might already be part of the business, and it could make sense for them to step into their parent's shoes and take over as a partner. Or the owner's children, whether adults are not, may have no interest in being part of the business and are simply looking for compensation as part of their parent's estate.

A Buy/Sell Agreement can easily be modified over time, so that it is always the right fit for the partners. That's why the relationship with an estate planner has to be an on-going thing, and not a one-shot deal. The estate planner should be there to implement changes as the partner's lives change.

6 More Complicated Family Situations

We have covered different ways for business owners to protect their family and deal with succession of their business. We've talked about the different types of business entities and the different options for the way that a business owner can pass the business down to his family, or at the very least, pass down the monetary value of the business.

Now, let's address some of the specific "out of the box" issues that some business owners face, but may be different from the norm.

Part I
Blended Families

First, let's address business owners that have blended families, because there are special considerations when it comes to business owners that may be on a second or third marriage.

It's not uncommon for a business owner, or any client really, to get married, have children, and then get divorced later. Sometimes they get remarried and it's not always a great friendship between the first spouse and the second spouse.

When it comes to business owners passing down their business and their other assets to their family, most business owners agree that they want their children, if they have any, to be the beneficiaries of the business, whether it's the proceeds of a business sale or taking over the business themselves. In those situations, they still want to take care of the spouse as well. We therefore need to take special care with the way that the business and other assets are passed to the children and/or spouse.

First, if the business owner drafts a standard Last Will that leaves everything to her spouse from the second marriage, then he (the spouse) would be her sole beneficiary and there is no guarantee that he would use the proceeds for anything other than himself. He could easily exclude the business owner's children from the prior marriage.

In most cases, the situation we want to avoid is when we leave discretion with the second spouse. It can be easy for the second spouse to rationalize not giving anything to the children from the first marriage, especially if there are children of the second marriage as well. If the business owner wants to make sure that the business owner's children from the first marriage receive a share of inheritance, it's better not to leave things to the second spouse's decision.

At the same time, we don't want to completely skip over the second spouse and leave everything directly to the children either. The second spouse could then be left out in the cold when it comes to receiving assets and could potentially even get kicked out of his own home if that home belonged to the business owner, and everything is left to the kids.

In fact, there have been litigated cases in Massachusetts, where a business owner left his estate to his children but gave, so he thought, his second spouse the right to live in the house for her lifetime. He went online and used discount documents from a famous on-line legal drafting website, and those documents proved to be ineffective under Mass. Law. Because the documents were basically junk, the lifetime rights he intended to grant to his spouse were not valid. The children, who were adults at the time, were able to evict the second wife and sell the home, leaving the second spouse with nothing!

Now, it's possible that the second spouse in that case may have had a claim for what is called "equitable relief". That's when someone alleges that they have a claim, based on the concept of fairness, to part of the house. This is especially common if she made mortgage payments or otherwise contributed to the value of the home. She may even make an argument based on the "intent" of the deceased business owner, as an attempt to have the court make a ruling based on what she alleges the business owner wanted. At this point we don't know if she intends to file one of those claims to potentially get the share, but even if she does make the claim, and wins, we are still talking about potential years of litigation, and huge amounts of dollars in attorney fees. It all could have been avoided had the estate planning been done correctly.

Part II
QTIP Trusts

Continuing with the example of a business owner on a second or third marriage, with children from a first marriage, we have to consider the age of the business owner's children. If the business owner intends to leave the business assets to his children, but they are minors, then their guardian would have full authority over all of their assets with no oversight whatsoever. That means that he would essentially be turning the business over to his ex-spouse. That ex-spouse could sell the business, take all the proceeds and keep them for himself or herself and not provide anything for the children. So how do we solve those problems?

The best way is with the QTIP Trust. I know it's a funny name, and it stands for Qualified Terminable Interest Property Trust. That's legalese mumbo jumbo for saying that the individual can provide assets to someone for the duration of his or her lifetime and then have those assets pass to a secondary beneficiary when the first beneficiary dies.

In our example, if we've got a business owner who is on her second marriage and has children from a first marriage, she can use the QTIP Trust to leave assets to the second spouse, for his lifetime, to make sure that he is taken care of. But we aren't giving the second spouse the right to decide what happens to those assets if he were to pass away – in other words, he has the use of the assets for his life, but then they automatically transfer to beneficiaries named in the QTIP

Trust. Those lifetime assets can include a lifetime interest in the house and can potentially include a lifetime interest in the business or the business ownership (stock, LLC interest).

The QTIP Trust provides that when the second spouse passes away, the assets then could flow to the business owner's child or children from the first marriage. We've made sure the second spouse is taken care of, but don't have to worry about him/her disinheriting the business owner's children from the first marriage. Note that, if the children are minors at the time, the QTIP Trust prescribes that the assets will be administered by a trustee for the benefit of the children until they are old enough. By having the trustee in charge, we wouldn't have to worry about the kids' guardian, who is likely the first spouse, having control of those assets.

The QTIP Trust avoids any potential conflict of interest with the first spouse or the first spouse taking charge of the assets because the business owner would name an independent trustee to handle the purse strings. If the children are adults, they could receive their share outright.

Note that the QTIP Trust does not have to be an all or nothing solution. In other words, all of the business owner's assets don't need to pass through the QTIP Trust. It's possible that the business owner could leave the marital home to his second spouse outright, or he could leave it to her for her lifetime, with the property going to the children upon her passing and leave it out of the QTIP. He could also deal specifically with the business assets and run them through the QTIP Trust. Or if the children are adults, he could leave those assets directly to the children, but run other assets through the QTIP to avoid the issue of the second spouse failing to include the children from the previous marriage.

There can be an even bigger problem if there are children from both marriages, because the second spouse is typically inclined to protect his or her *own children* (the children of the second marriage) versus making sure that the children of the first marriage are included. In that case, there can be an even bigger chance that the children from the first marriage will be disinherited if we give all the assets to the second spouse. The QTIP Trust solves all of those problems.

As an added bonus, the QTIP Trust provides estate tax protection as well. The QTIP Trust helps the business owner to preserve the maximum estate tax exemption in the same way that the credit shelter Trust does, but it goes the extra step that allows the business owner to designate the (1) lifetime beneficiaries and (2) the final beneficiaries. This means that the assets are used for one beneficiary during his or her lifetime, and then ultimately passed to secondary beneficiaries after the death of the primary beneficiary. This is an extremely valuable tool when your estate planner knows how to use it.

THE QTIP TRUST ELIMINATES THE CHANCE OF ANYONE BEING DISINHERITED

Very often, novice attorneys or "dabblers" -- those who dabble in estate planning but don't specialize in it -- either don't know that a QTIP Trust even exists or they don't know how to draft it or use it properly. It is something that is very easily overlooked, and it can be the perfect solution when done right. We get the estate tax exemption, which is great, but we also make sure that all children or other beneficiaries of the business owner are taken care of properly and no one is excluded.

7 Long-term Care

Part I

Life Insurance with a Chronic Illness Rider for Long-Term Care

Business Owners need to pay special attention to how they will pay for their long-term care. I tell my clients that I understand why they don't want to talk about long-term care, because no one wants to talk about it, but the fact is that, unless something else gets us first, we are ALL going to need some form of long-term care, whether it's care in the home or in assisted living or in a nursing home facility.

When it comes to long-term care, there are only three ways to pay:

The first is through long-term care insurance or life insurance with a chronic illness rider. One of the best ways to pay for long-term care is with some form of insurance policy that provides long-term care coverage.

The second way to pay is to pay out-of-pocket, meaning that you would spend your assets on your long-term care, paying out-of-pocket at the "private pay" rates set by the facility. This is the most expensive option, and assets can dwindle very quickly with private pay.

The third option is to position your assets so that you can qualify for Medicaid. Medicaid not only provides coverage for long-term care, but they pay facilities at special rates that are a lot cheaper than private pay rates.

The downside to Medicaid is that it's possible for Medicaid to put a lien against assets of someone receiving long-term care benefits, and Medicaid collects money back from a benefit-recipient's estate upon their passing.

Regardless of the drawbacks, the money that Medicaid has paid out is paid out at their discounted rate, as opposed to the private pay rate, making the lien much smaller than if you were to use your own assets and pay monthly at the private-pay rate.

A common misconception from business owners is that they make too much money to qualify for Medicaid. Often times, on paper, they do make too much money and have too many assets. Medicaid is an asset-based benefit, meaning that if you have assets in excess of their limit, you either have to spend down your assets or you don't qualify. However, through the use of proper estate planning techniques, we can get individuals qualified even if they have more assets than what is allowed by Medicaid. The right estate planning lawyer can position your assets to qualify for Medicaid, *even if you've got more money and assets than the guidelines allow.*

Part II
Medicaid Protection of the Home

Positioning assets for Medicaid eligibility is done in a few different ways, with several estate planning tools. The two primary tools are Trusts, which sometimes we refer to as Medicaid Trusts, and the second way is through annuities.

First let's focus on the Medicaid Trust. We can use Medicaid Trusts to protect the business owner's assets. Be warned, this is a very, very complicated Trust. It has to be done perfectly, and it has to comply with Medicaid's regulations, so it is a very, very technical document. This is something that needs to be done right the first time and not something that should be done by any lawyer other than a specialist. For that reason, it costs, and you should expect to pay a premium for this Trust. The assets protected will far outweigh any up-front costs. This Trust can be used to hold assets, including real estate and investment properties. It can be used to hold cash as well.

To protect real estate, the property is placed into this Trust and the Trust is designed to pass to business owner's beneficiaries upon his or her passing. However, the additional benefit to this Trust is that any property put in there can be protected from Medicaid liens after the property has been in the Trust for five years. That's because Medicaid has what is called the five year look back. On the day you apply for benefits, they look back at the previous five years' transactions, and if they can determine that you gave money away or made a gift, which would include a transfer to a Trust, they can penalize you and assess a penalty period. If the penalty period is assessed, you have to rescind the gift and now the assets are back in your name.

In 2020, and in 2021, that look back period is five years, and when it comes to these Medicaid Trusts, we look at it as "the sooner, the better". We want to get the five-year clock running long *before* the business owner is in need of long-term care. If we do it far enough ahead, then the property placed into these Trusts, can be protected after five years, and the assets are not counted as assets by Medicaid. That means they cannot be subject to Medicaid liens and they can't be counted towards a Medicaid asset limit.

It's a versatile and useful tool, when drafted properly and used properly. Sadly, many non-specialist estate planners make mistakes with this, and I very often have to be the bearer of bad news, when I have to tell a family that property they thought was protected in Trust, is not protected at all. They think that they have surpassed that five-year clock, and then I have to tell them that the five-year clock never actually started, because of bad provisions in the Trust document.

Part III
Medicaid Annuities

The other tool that we use to help position assets for Medicaid qualification are Medicaid compliant annuities. What the annuity allows us to do is take a lump sum of money that is in the business owner's name and move some of that cash into a Medicaid compliant annuity.

Medicaid looks at assets and they look at income. These two categories determine the way Medicaid views your financial situation. Because Medicaid is asset-based, there is a set asset limit, and if you've got assets over that limit, you don't qualify. But by setting up the annuity and dropping a lump sum of cash into the annuity, what we've done is we've taken a lump sum cash asset and converted it, by putting it into the annuity. The annuity pays out over time, so we've changed it from an asset into an income stream, and therefore taken that cash out of the calculation that Medicaid uses to determine your total assets.

In their most basic form, these Medicaid annuities are an insurance product where a certain lump sum cash is paid into an insurance company and the insurance company pays that money back, plus interest, over time via monthly payments. Logistically, we've taken cash out of the bank, paid it over to an annuity and now we don't have that cash sitting in the bank anymore and it can't be counted as an asset. The annuity company is paying back monthly payments to the business owner who's in need of long-term care. The business owner can use those monthly payments to pay toward their long-term care, and the funds can be used towards their copayment (or as Medicaid calls it a PPA, which stands for patient paid amount).

The other advantage with the annuity is that we've gotten the business owner qualified for Medicaid immediately, so that Medicaid is paying the facility at their lower Medicaid rate and not the private pay rate. That way, we get that lump sum cash to last much, much longer. And we've taken someone that would not have qualified for Medicaid because of their assets, spent down their assets by converting into the annuity, and now we've got them under the asset limit to the point where they can qualify.

Medicaid Trusts and annuities are among the most useful tools when it comes to positioning yourself to qualify for Medicaid and protecting your assets. But again, these tools are easily misunderstood and mismanaged.

Both tools are highly important and effective for business owners because business owners often own assets as part of the business, whether it's equipment, computers, real estate, or other types of assets. The business owner has to take special care when looking at how they're going to afford their long-term care.

Part IV
Long-Term Care Insurance and Chronic Illness Riders

At the start of this chapter, we went over the three ways to pay for long-term care. The first way was through insurance, and it's time to take a deeper dive into the insurance option for long-term care.

There are different types of insurance policies that can be used to pay for a long-term care. The first is the traditional long-term care insurance policy, which I must admit in the current state of things, I'm not a fan of.

In the past, the only insurance product and the only type of policy that could be used to pay for long-term care was the traditional long-term care insurance policy. People that have long-term care policies from years back didn't have any other options at the time. Those policies tend to be expensive and they can *only be used to pay for long-term care.* They have various limits, meaning there is a limit they will pay out per month. There's also a limit they'll pay out per year, as well as an overall policy limit, meaning that when this overall dollar amount has been paid out, the coverage stops completely.

Even if you have a long-term care insurance policy, they typically are not sufficient to cover all long-term care costs and shouldn't be used as an excuse to fail to plan for long-term care. This is especially true if the policy was taken out a long time ago, because not all policies include cost of living adjustments and the cost of long-term care today is many, many times higher than it was 15 to 20 years ago. I often see clients with long-term care insurance policies that they think are all set, and when I review their coverage, I find it woefully inadequate. Even if you have one of these policies, a specialist estate planning attorney that is educated in insurance as well should review it to tell you exactly what you have.

The other negative thing about these long-term care policies is that if you pay in for years and years, and you never go into long-term care because you pass away from a heart attack or stroke first, and never get into long- term care, the benefit is lost. You don't get anything, your estate doesn't get anything, and your family doesn't get anything. Even though you may have paid in tens of thousands of dollars and even more into this policy, if you don't need long-term care or you never make it to long-term care, the policy is void at your death and the insurance company keeps all the money.

TRADITIONAL LONG-TERM CARE INSURANCE, HAS NO DEATH BENEFIT

Instead of the traditional long-term care policy, a newer option, and one that I like better, is a life insurance policy with what's called a chronic illness rider. What the chronic illness rider does is allows us to borrow against the death benefit of the life insurance policy to make payments for long-term care. If you have a life insurance policy with a chronic illness rider, that is for example, $100,000, you can borrow against that policy, use the money to pay for long-term care, and when you pass away, there is a death benefit for any funds not used towards long-term care that gets paid to your family.

The other great thing about this policy, which distinguishes it from the traditional long-term care policy, is that if you pass away without ever going into long-term care, your family gets the death benefit.

Unlike the traditional long-term care insurance, which has no death benefit and no benefit whatsoever if you don't need long-term care, a life insurance policy with a chronic illness rider is still a life insurance policy. If you don't need long-term care, the death benefit is paid to your beneficiaries. If you do need long-term care, you borrow against the policy value, to pay for long-term care. And you pass whatever's left, whatever hasn't been paid out for long-term care, that death benefit goes to the beneficiaries. There's no fear or issue with paying into the policy for years and no one ever getting anything back.

Part V
Supplemental Needs Trusts (SNT)

Special considerations need to be taken for business owners that have children with different or special needs. In most cases, business owners make too much money for a special needs child to receive many government benefits. If the business owner passes away and leaves everything to their disabled child directly, their inherited assets will be counted against the child and they won't be entitled to any asset-based government benefit. The way around that is through use of what we call either a special needs Trust or a supplemental needs Trust, a/k/a the SNT.

What those Trusts allow us to do is to have the business owner leave assets intended for the disabled child to this SNT Trust. The Trust is written in such a way that it does not disqualify the child from government benefits. The Trust funds, if used properly, are not counted against the child as an asset when applying for benefits.

At the same time, the Trustee can use the money in the Trust on behalf of the disabled child in such a way that it does not disqualify them for government benefits, but still supplements anything that government benefits don't cover. The key is that the Trust money cannot be used for anything that the government benefit would otherwise pay for. If the disabled child has assistance for paying their rent, then the Trust can't be used to also pay rent. In other words, the funds in the Trust are designed to supplement the government benefit, not supplant that benefit. If the disabled child is paying $1,000 a month in rent and has a government benefit for $500, the Trust can pay the difference as a supplemental amount -- the Trust can pay that $500 in rent that was not covered through the government benefit.

As long as there is no overlap between what the Trust pays for and what the government pays for, the assets can't be counted against the disabled child when determining their eligibility for benefits. Again, this is something that is very often overlooked by novice estate planners. They don't know how to write these Trusts properly or how they have to be administered so that the benefits are not denied.

Part VI
Standalone Retirement Trusts (SRT)

Business owners have to be cognizant of their retirement plans and what will happen with their retirement if they were to pass away. This is an especially important point for business owners that may be divorced or on a second marriage and have children from that first marriage. The business owner may not want the first spouse to receive benefits from his retirement plan. But if the children are minors, that ex-spouse would have control over the assets, as guardian for the minor children.

Instead, we can utilize what is called a standalone retirement Trust (the SRT). This Trust dictates what happens with your retirement money when you pass, and it can make sure that a trustee uses the money on behalf of the beneficiaries, which in this example would be the children from the first marriage. The trust would not allow any control by the first spouse. At the same time, the retirement Trust makes provisions for any required minimum distributions that may have to be paid out. The Trust dictates specifically what will happen with them when they are paid from the retirement company, and whether they are to pass directly to the beneficiaries or whether they are to stay in the Trust.

Under the new Secure Act that was enacted in 2020, the payout periods for these retirement plans have changed. In most cases, retirement funds have to be fully paid out within a 10-year period. That means if there are young beneficiaries, the beneficiaries could have to start receiving the money while they are still minors, which again would put control with the guardian, who is oftentimes the first spouse.

Instead, the retirement Trust can hold those distributions from the retirement plan. That way, even after the 10-year period, the Trust can go on administering the property for the beneficiaries until they reach a certain age or ages at which time the money is paid out. The ex-spouse would have no opportunity to control the funds.

8 Marketing for Business Owners

The last thing I want to touch on is marketing for business owners. Our services at our office go beyond standard estate planning. Yes, we do address estate planning, elder planning, life insurance and annuities, but we also address the overall health of our client's businesses.

It happens very often that a client might be an excellent service provider, might be a great accountant, a great electrician, a great financial advisor, but is not necessarily great at marketing their business, especially with a small business that either has a single owner or only two or three partners. They are so focused on providing the services that they are hired for that they don't remember to take time to market their business.

We offer business marketing consulting services to our clients to make sure that they are maximizing their profits, spending their time in the appropriate way and getting the word out to the community about their services. See the last page of this book for a word from Monteforte Law, P.C.'s

Chief Marketing Officer, Nicole Rego, and FREE information about these services.

You could be the best carpenter in the world, but if no one knows you exist, then you aren't doing anyone any favors. Not you or the clients that could use your services. We can provide an analysis of your current marketing at no charge.

9 Final Thoughts

In conclusion, while estate planning is something that is important for everyone, there are numerous special considerations that need to be taken into account when dealing with business owners.

Business owners have unique needs, unique problems, and require unique solutions. Business assets are a special kind of asset in which the business owner has worked to earn these assets and wants to keep them away from the government and keep them with their families and their beneficiaries. An experienced estate planner can help business owners to provide adequately for their families to make sure that there is no question about what will happen to the business if a business owner passes away and also make sure that taxes are minimized.

This is not something that should be taken lightly or that should be back-burnered for another day. As soon as a company or a small business starts offering goods or services and their business now legally exists, that is the time to deal with the estate planning and business succession. However, it's never too late, even if your business has been going strong for 10 or 20 years. But if you don't have these documents in place, it's very important that you do so right away.

My last piece of advice is to make sure you are dealing with an attorney that specializes in this work. Don't go to someone who dabbles. The potential pitfalls, penalties and taxes are far too much to risk. Keep the business in your family, minimize taxes, protect your beneficiaries.

You've worked hard to start and grow your business. Now you need to protect it. The right estate plan will keep the business assets in your family and protect your family's future.

Get a FREE Marketing Analysis

Now a word from Monteforte Law, P.C.'s Chief Marketing Officer, Nicole Rego:

Marketing is not as easy as it sounds. It is actually very complex and has multiple levels to it. In order to make your business and yourself successful, you need to face marketing head on and do it well.

There is a lot more to marketing than just making a simple advertisement for a newspaper or creating a social media post and calling it a day. To be successful, you need to have a basic understanding of how marketing truly works, and the areas to focus on. So, that leads me to the most basic question out there…what is marketing?

In the simplest of terms, marketing is the action of promoting your services or products in hopes of driving profitable customer action. However, that is easier said than done. Marketing ranges in all types of forms. You can market online, in print, by word-of-mouth, through education and so much more. The ways to market are ever-changing and it seems like every day there is a new way to get your product and service out there. Despite the way you choose to market, one thing remains at the highest importance. This one thing is your content.

You may have heard the phrase "Content is King" and if you haven't you better get familiar with it. Content marketing is what drives those profitable customers to you and your business. The main goals behind content marketing are to build an audience, establish authority and, lastly, drive sales. People want to be educated, not sold to. So, your content must be educational to be successful. When your content begins to educate the right audience at the right time, sales will follow. Once again, this is much harder than it sounds. These three steps can never be accomplished if you do not know what you are doing!

Now that you know the importance of content, it is important to know how to create it. Your content should be specific to you and your products or services. Always create content that is based off your business so that the people who are looking at it are the right clients and people you want reaching out. After you create this content you have to put it out into the world. Content can be distributed through numerous channels. Some of the best ways to release your content include writing blogs, creating videos, email marketing, direct mail, and of course, social media marketing. You want to release your content to your ideal client in as many formats as possible and do it regularly.

The world of marketing is always changing, and it is changing fast. If you want to stay competitive, you need to keep up. Good thing we can help with that! As Michael mentioned earlier, we not only offer help in the estate planning and elder law world, we can now offer you help on your overall business. If you want to see how effective your marketing is in today's world, I would be happy to give you a FREE assessment, just for reading this book! I am currently the Chief Marketing Officer at Monteforte Law, P.C. and in addition to this I received my bachelor's degree in Marketing. I know what I am talking about and I know what makes good marketing. Since we changed the way we do marketing at our law office, we were able to triple our sales. The impact the right marketing has is astronomical.

Marketing cannot be something you try without doing your research. You must be educated on the topic in order to be successful at it, just like anything else in life. So, that's why we are here to help. We want to educate you and help you jump start your marketing so you can get a jump start on your future.

FOR MORE INFORMATION AND A FREE ANALYSIS OF YOUR MARKETING VISIT:

MYMARKETINGANALYSIS.COM

MONTEFORTE LAW, P.C.

FAMILY • LEGACY • SECURITY

400 Tradecenter, Suite 6890
Woburn, MA 01801

Phone: **978-657-7437**

WWW.MONTEFORTELAW.COM

WA

Made in the USA
Monee, IL
04 November 2026

67381840R10056